The Sum of Us

POEMS BY WOMEN WHO WRITE

Ella Eytan ~ Laurel Feigenbaum ~ Melanie Maier

Angelika Quirk ~ Gabrielle Rilleau

Contents

Melanie Maier

Angelika Quirk

Gabrielle Rilleau

Foreword

Full disclosure: I have known almost all of these lyrical ladies and their work for a long time, so I'm unabashedly biased. And what strikes me in this collection is their admirable confrontation and transcendence of the dark forces we are heir to. Though the president's tweets "spin truth to dust," and a honeymoon begins in a leaky boat, and Death leaves eight hundred pairs of "empty shoes . . . ashore," and the beloved continue to leave us (one way or another), these poets are intimate with the imperatives of life, of savoring it for all it's worth.

In these pages you'll find the mind seeking a companionable partner in the body, and the body that will brook no truce with the mind when it comes to all-out embracing the sensual. That embrace is not only sexual; it is large, it contains multitudes, ranging from an ancient love of the sea to the perspective of flying at a high altitude, to the love of musical words, to the cherishing of parents and partners. The spirit surveys all it apprehends and wants to let it all in. The memorial candle on the mantel does not go out. The dying mother and attending daughter speak only of life. The largest orange on the tree is picked and carried into the house "like the sun after a dreary day."

Thomas Centolella
Marin County, California
September 2019

To be a poet is a condition, not a profession.

Robert Graves (1895-1985)

The Sum of Us

Ella Eytan

"Vast, that ocean—sudden winds, storms."
from *Possession*

Solstice

Late afternoon sun
lights the edges
of every bush and tree,
the rest left
in shadow.

This is the time
of the honing down
of each day
and something in me wears away—
simplifies
like the season.
cold scentless air summons
fewer images,
layered clothes muffle touch.

Without summer's profusion
I see what's essential—
you, the purity of you,
your rock-hard presence here
in the center.
Simply that.

Dark Wakening

In a rumple of sheets,
blanket pushed down,
the night's chill,
hard on my arm,
tugs me

from my effort
against a wind pulling
my rudderless boat
far from shore.

I wake and find you
warm and still,
your breath lifting
hairs on my arm.

You turn. I snuggle
stomach to back,
leg to leg
and wind my arm over
to touch your chest.

Struggle loosens
and my breath slows
to match yours.
Your presence a gift
these many years.

Love Poem

A canopy of sycamores
touch overhead,
skewed limbs
reaching skyward
as if in supplication.

In summer,
enormous leaves flapping,
you can almost believe.
But autumn
shuts down the fountains.
A flare of yellow
nips at green
and everything slips
to earth,
into slumber,
the dark umber
of the soul.

I can never
love you enough.

Your Hands

Ah, love,
when I lift
your hand like this
and kiss each finger
that loves me so well,
I want to tell
them with my tongue
and teeth
how I love their feel—
hairs fine and red,
wide soft pads
at the tips,
slight roughness there,
even the nails
short and square.
Your hands
talk with their touch.
I listen to them
with my skin
that wants so much.

After You Left

The air
rearranged itself
around your absence—
hint of your familiar scent,
rim of a glass still warm
from your lips.

And where, on the table,
your elbow rested,
the faintest glint of light.
Not solid, not you,

all that is left.

Tomato

Red tomato on a white ribbed plate, Tasty Tom, but misnamed. Actually female. And royal with its six-pointed green crown, nattily bent, casually elegant. And sensual. A small tear, and juice gathers at the lip like the first blood shed with the moon's passing. When I spread the lips wide they are like the inside of all women—the flesh exposed, an offering. I see how men love us, we are so open and real. And I can see how women love women, the flesh of the other opened, a reflection, again and again. I suck out pulp, liquid and seeds, the skin is yellow as the sun, taken down and spread thin, even as we take the sun and darken to a golden hue. Take this red globe of summer into your mouth unconditionally, it is the best way. Bite into it so that each nuance of flesh opens in tiny explosions. Most of all, pay attention. Bite deep enough, and you bite back out into the world.

Possession

I am fresh-tossed hay,
steam rising
from the flanks of cows
on a cold day.
I'm the salt lick
at the pastures edge,
the tongue that hollows it.

I am translucent
as the snail,
belly muscles rippling
as I row across a lit window.

I am many chambered—
a nautilus. Your hand
could span my sensuous curve.
Lift me to your ear,
there is the sea in me.
Can you hear?

Vast, that ocean—
sudden winds, storms.
It is inevitable—
the night's first hint of light,
then that pencil line
of trouble
before the dawn.

The Habit of Beauty

I don't find each wrinkle
a badge of good character.
Instead, concealer,
loose clothes cover
a multitude of sins.

I'm perversely drawn
to young men—
taut muscles, clear skin.
I try to blame the media,
the youth culture. But,

when I dig deep,
the attraction seems encoded.
It's for the next generation—
no shutoff valve.
It's what the genes want.

Depends on the Angle

Fall rains have laid
a wash of green over fields,
soft shades that elbow through
gray beards of dead grass.

Wind parts the new green
this way and that
changing color the way velvet,
stroked at different angles,
alters the sheen.

On a distant ribbon of road,
a parade of cars
you know are speeding,
seem to go in slow motion.

Black and white cows
dot hills
that roll on forever.
They bend to eat—
an ancient rhythm of the fields.

Stare long enough and you
could join them, forget
who you are, become part
of a dream
the earth has of itself.

Ants and the Spider

Three ants have wandered
for days, lost
on my bathroom sink.
This is their desert—
a lost scent-trail
not shifting dunes.

They run briefly up the wall
but always return.
It is, if painful,
at least familiar.

Where tub meets floor,
a sticky web.
Just under it,
a litter of exoskeletons.
Yet ants remain masters
of their subterranean domain.

Perhaps I let them remain
as a window into nature
in my ordered house.
Or that I've learned
to observe closely
so affection floods in—
that small but marvelous
similarity
between them and me.

By the Sea

The sea rolls steadily in.
I become ancient, spineless
as kelp swaying
to its rhythm.

I want always to be this loose,
to float
effortlessly as a moon jelly.
Mostly I squat
like mottled rock,
damp, salt-stained,
a horny toad become stone.

I want to be sea-witched,
feathered
with bone-white sand, `
to let kelp-scented breezes
chill my skin.
I want to let it all in

and open to the killdeer
calling from the dunes, to sand
whispering
as it lifts in the wind.

I want voices drifting
across the beach
to detach from their stories and
without need,
seep into me whole.

My Mind

descends
now and then
to join my body
when it tires
of solo tripping,
the witty whittling
of whole into concept,
evaluations,
the endless
verbal peregrinations.

It wants company
in its wanderings,
wants to feel
the sensible brevity
of blood and bone.
It wants a home
in the beat
of moving feet,
the anchor
of soil.
It wants,
no, it needs,
the corporeal.

My Body

now and then needs sensation—
sun's soothing warmth,
breezes riffling hair,
music,
rhythm of waves.

I crave the poetry
of touch—
skin stroked
by hands slightly rough,
hair caressed
with the softest brush.

My body wants to ask
(is it too much?)
for the rasp of tongue
in intimate places,
blurred, unfocused eyes
on male faces.
My body wants
what it wants,
unfettered, let loose,
overruling the mind,
not even a truce.

Renoir at Seventy-five

They tied a brush
to his arthritic hands
so he could paint near the sea
for air's countless moisture-mirrors
and for grasses that shake
their skirts in a slow swish and dazzle.

Through a thick soup of light
his models danced
trailing scarves of lapis and amber,
alabaster skin blurred at the edges
into soft blue and violet.

Parasols of lemon and jade,
pistachio and persimmon followed
in loops and arcs as they spun.

He took it all in,
his brush recording motion and stillness,
a curve here, a slash of darkness
to move it forward.

He painted,
drunk on sun and breeze, color
and the opulence of flesh,
untouchable now
except with his brush.

Rainforest, Olympic Peninsula

There are things a forest can tell you
when you are quiet
and know a little of its language.
Old Red Cedar, still half-nude
as they left her, tells of ancient people—
her bark peeled for clothing and baskets.
In a litter of stumps and vines
mushrooms fluff their caps in the damp.
Their bright tongues broadcast
pleasure or poison in equal measure.

In her loose bark, giant Sitka
gathers hemlock seeds that sprout
on her trunk and send roots down
to solid ground. They'll stand
on rooty tiptoes when old Sitka goes.

The great trees are busy in their slow way
giving food and shelter to animals that dart
like shadow beneath their branches.

The forest awakens from sleep.
Moist and mirrored ferns uncurl—
lady, maidenhair, even old liverwort
down by the stream, all that darkness
a dream the whole forest walks into
and out of. And the ancient ones?
You can almost see them
rise up in columns of steam.

Mill Valley

Once summer cottages, our houses
have become boxes that lean
over lot lines spilling out husbands,
children and wives in the rhythm
of rush hour.
Cars weave through traffic
elbowing curbs in their SUV's.

The street shimmers, fata morgana,
just ahead as I drive.
A red Escalade cuts in front,
flips me a tail pipe. A few hot days
and goodbye civility. I yearn
for familiar ideas—friendly neighbors,
a certain measured pace.

At last my driveway.
Wind pours through the eucalyptus
in great cataracts of sound.
Fog will follow.
Privet and oleander begin
to natter. Birds unpin
from power lines that define our view,
wheel up and scatter.

October

A slow rain
polishes pavement,
privets slicked and shining.

Summer has her hand in
but it's slipping,
broad leaves edged
in gold and red.

People walking by
tilt their heads
toward the sidewalk
as if they could learn

from that geography
of fissures and cracks
why good things
eventually turn,

why the very gift
that makes
everything grow
feels like loss.

Gratitude

Raccoons maraud my fishpond
to feast, quail cluck and peck in dirt
and a fox raised three kits
by my lemon tree. I watched them
leap among my vegetables,
climb trees playing how to survive.

Needing lemons, foxes nearby,
I walked slowly, babies scampering away.
Talking softly to the mother,
I said "Don't worry, I won't hurt you."
She remained calm as the fruit.

When the kits were almost grown
she nursed them, watching me
watching her.
They lay on their backs, pulling
on the teats, stretching hind legs,
pushing on their mother's belly
like a human baby, like a gift.

Later, we found a dead rat
on our front deck.
Fox gratitude.
They are gone now,
but I have this poem.
Some gifts keep on giving.

Old Swimming Hole

The pond holds the sky
and an intense green
below the overhanging willow.
A bobolink punctures silence.

It's spring,
wildflowers and strawberries,
breeze-ruffled grass. Perfection.
Did I see this at age ten or eleven?

Cows grazed upstream,
excrement floating down
to our swimming hole.
Thick bloom of algae,
soft mud ooze on the bottom.
Farm kids aren't fussy.

Once, cousin Adrian dove off the bank,
only his legs visible above the water.
He was buried so deep in muck
I could barely pull him up.
Ever since, between us, a bond.

In spring melt, the pond
spreads wide over its banks,
broken sticks of bushes spiking through.
Ducks careen and splash,
drunk with abundance
and the joy of return.

When Mother Died

When the call traveled
two thousand miles to my kitchen
it divided time
into before and after.

Cold started where my arm
rested against the counter
and spread, the words
like rain falling—
accident, wing of the door,
swept under, car careening down.

Words dissolved in the downpour—
thunder, lightning, darkness.
What was meant
pinned unchanging, unchangeable
on the walls.

In the plane, looking down, it was
as it always was,
sun lighting clouds below,
people wrapped in their problems,

everyone going on as usual,
the world going on, while I
flew inexorably toward
what was no longer there.

Laurel Feigenbaum

"*Open the earth to enclose me, change my form.*"
Daphne to her father, the river god,
from *Mating Call*

Double Delight

Seduced by scent and voluptuous bloom,
I succumbed to cultivating a rose garden
unaware the nurturing required was like
the care and feeding of children.

Yes, there's the joy of *Just Joey* —
frilled petals in a blend of copper and apricot,
the velvet brown of *Hot Cocoa,* the clean
green leaves and white clusters of *Iceberg.*

But then there's *Double Delight* —
outer ivory petals stained crimson with the sun,
heraldic symbol of the War of the Roses to be won
again in the fight against black spot, rust, mildew.

Pellets of systemic fungicide, vaccinations,
injections, sprays of herbicide,
Rose Defense, Miracle-Gro, mulch.
Deleafing the contagious before they drop,
dead heading.

By summer's end, despite the Bard,
Othello stands upright, strong, thorny,
the darkest of red roses. *Ophelia* has survived
her watery grave, alights lovely as ever,
blush white, exquisitely formed and fragrant.
Perhaps she is the harlot Hamlet thought she was
having produced more than thirty offspring,
sported them in her virginal innocence.

Weekends, Sea Ranch

Early morning and late afternoon walks
through damp meadows or along the bluff,
the Pacific crashing a rocky shore,
exploding through the blowhole
only to settle back quietly into white foam caps
before repeating.

Pillowed by cushions of carpet grass,
our backs against the berm,
we watch osprey dive,
their catch between strong talons
carried on thermals to the ridge above.
On shell beach, a silver-white arabesque of sanderlings
chases the tide twisting left then right at water's edge,
a mud-quest for mollusks interrupted by
boisterous children.

At low tide we pry mussels from rocks
to mix with garlic, wine, hot pots of pasta, laughter and talk,
the sunset framed in picture windows.
Later, on the perch you built, a million stars overhead,
the moon shining on the water,
wind swirling round us,
we listen for the rhythm of waves against shore,
cry of the oystercatcher, restless cormorants settling in.

Weather Report

Drapes open this morning
to flooding sun
after days and nights of cold gray rain.
Life in motion again—

Walkers back on the path,
children's voices, dogs, bikes.
A mockingbird ventures forth,
surveys from the fence.

Finches dart from acacia
to a makeshift birdbath,
vying for puddle space.

The bower vine that suffered
winter freeze is green
with energy to climb;
not so, the bougainvillea.

We needed rain,
all but danced for it,
feel guilty if we complain.
But, oh, the sun—

Sociology

To say we were passing acquaintances
would be too thin
or that we were friends, too thick.

She married a thick stack of old money.
I married and worked.
She volunteered, her picture often featured
in Sunday's *Style* section.

Somewhere along the way
we were on a board together.
After a meeting, I admitted
to finding the proceedings boring.
By the time the elevator reached ground zero,
I knew she considered me
entirely too thin.

Not long ago over a buffet table
and after the usual greetings, she asked
what I'd been doing.
I confessed to poetry, reading
and even some writing.
Curious, she looked up.

Being attracted to words and wordplay
since the first time I heard
"petroleum" as I sat in a large chair
with my small ear tuned to the radio.
My latest loves: *tintinnabulation*
and *glossolalia.*

My stock visibly rising
with the transformative power
of poetry and each mellifluous sound
and syllable.

Donatello's *David*

Imprisoned in the Bargello
in the heart of historic Florence
the young bronze *David* stands alone,
a runway model ready to be admired
from across the second floor gallery.

Slim, youthful body posed,
clothed only in cocked hat and sandals;
a sure foot resting on the severed head
and helmet of the vanquished Philistine
as if it were all in a day's work,
a mere stone's throw from the ordinary.

The soft curves of his molded body,
dreamy grace, slight smile, and
plume of feathers from Goliath's helmet
that stroke his inner thigh
hide the hard metal that lies beneath.

He has not aged or tired these five hundred years,
bronze brightness neither dulled
nor diminished by his great marble image
a few blocks away.

Here no crowds wait in line.
No souvenir "giftshop" replica.
The mind will remember
youth's arrogance and beauty—
David not yet grown into his own Goliath.

Gertrude: The Stein Collection

"If I Told Him. A Complete Portrait of Picasso"
—Gertrude Stein, 1923

If he asked me if I liked it
If I told him would he like it?
Would he like it if I told him
the wheelchair was in the way?

Fine for my long-standing husband,
but I was pushing the chair,
suffering complaints about my driving,
warnings of near-missed ankles or shins,
and navigating for a front-row seat
before Picasso or Matisse
proved major distractions—

until we came to Gertrude
settled Buddha-like on a pedestal,
relaxed in the folds and creases
of her fully rounded bronze girth,
one shirt button left undone,
hands resting on a skirt pulled taut
across parted knees. Hair pulled back in a bun,
light reflecting from cheekbones and chin.

Leaning forward
as if she had something to confide,
inviting the viewer to linger, come closer,
caught in her gaze and sheer presence.

There was There there.

Matrimony

An elderly couple dies within hours
of each other. I think *How Sweet!*
I joke, speculate—pills? fatigue?
the power of angry words?
Natural causes aside, seventy years seems
unnatural, the dailyness of it—
an abstraction I can't get my head around.

And here we are—habits, routines,
wants, needs met and unmet,
six-and-a-half decades a day at a time.
Folding laundry, replenishing bananas
and hearing aid batteries. Sunday brunches,
the week's news, celebrations, memorials,
TV "remote" tug-of-wars,
accommodation, forgiveness.

I look into the same blue eyes
as he savors food, sucks chicken bones dry,
and so deliberately, head down, maneuvers
the walker around furniture to reach the bedside
where I'm propped up reading.
Leans over in his sagging underwear
for a goodnight kiss. *Sleep well.*

Laughter / Tears

We are complex creatures,
the sum of parts—
sometimes tender, sometimes tart,
pieced together with mettle
and a beating heart.

One day riding the waves,
another caught in an undertow.
I had a yellow Fiat once,
just like me—
all stop / all go.

Scholars question why.
Freud might blame it on mother,
a weak libido. or superego.
Some hold to fluoride, wind, stars,
Mercury in retrograde, Mars.

I for one consider
the push/pull of opposing forces
—whether by happenstance or plan—
to be our commonplace state
borne as best we can.

The Bed

In our first apartment we shared a Murphy wall bed
then graduated to a house and a queen,
framed Toulouse-Lautrec *The Kiss* positioned above:
a bedded couple face to face, wrapped in each other's arms,
a palette of yellow and red fading to pale blue, gray, green.
Fifty years later we visited them in the D'Orsey.

Quilts, linens, mattresses—firm, foam, orthopedic—
changed over the years, but *The Kiss* remained.
An electric blanket with dual controls, switched,
he turning the temperature down, me turning it up
through one long night.

Restless legs, trips to the bathroom, tossing, turning
for comfortable positions, waking, disturbing each other.
Then separate bedrooms.
Some mornings he visits me in the queen.

On a recent short vacation, we shared a king.
After one sleepless night, I moved four floors down,
the bed size of a Murphy and seven hours sleep.
Waking, I thought, I'll take the elevator to 812, lie down
beside him, talk of how we slept, what it was like to have
separate rooms, pretend we're under assumed
names in a clandestine affair. Young again.

The Memory of All That . . .

The way you wore your hat
all attitude and angle—
we'd swarm and swoon
when you'd croon,
Ol' Blue Eyes,
you make me feel so young.

Big band sounds of Tommy Dorsey,
trumpets blaring, hot drums, solo sax
and your mellow voice,
syncopated, upbeat, downbeat.

Couples swing, skirts flare,
feet to the beat, half-time, double-time,
on dance floors at the Palladium,
Earl Carroll's, USO Sundays
in Hollywood or Beverly Hills.

Just ahead, you and Ava Gardner walk
arm in arm up Beverly Drive—*Luck,
be a lady tonight*—and even though
I'm old and gray,
You make me feel so young.

Dancing 'round the kitchen table,
living room chairs, I swing and sway,
turn and twist, fingers snapping
in time to your timeless tune—
You make me feel so young.

Words and Music

If this were a practice life—

In the next
I'd croon and scat like Ella
Get down and dirty with Etta
Glide across the floor with Fred or Gene
Improvise with Basie
Score like Sondheim or Hammerstein.

In my spare time
I'd cultivate a garden
Be fluent in Spanish
Make soufflés like Julia
Lounge, putter, fritter,
Bask.

Like peanut butter
Have a big brother
Add a lover.

Message

Aristotle's disciple, Theophrastus,
sent a message in a bottle to prove
the Atlantic flowed into the Mediterranean.
Shipwrecked sailors sent messages
arriving too late for rescue.

Now from the Great Pacific Garbage Patch
castaway plastic bottles send messages
in languages foreign and domestic.
Societies' discards funneled from rivers,
storm drains, and ships at sea,
trapped in a confluence of currents,
a twice Texas-sized gyre of debris:

a stuffed bear, a lawn chair, toothbrushes,
plastic ware broken by sun and wind,
confetti-like particles, ingested,
mistaken for plankton;
chemical sludge passed in a chain
lantern fish to jellyfish to serving dish.

Whale bellies fill with fishing line,
sea lions strangle in trawl,
albatross choke, cry for rescue from the vortex
before we're all down the drain.

Mating Call

Seasonal breeders need no written rules,
their habits governed by climate, perpetuation
of species, reduced libido in off-season.

Other orders have other constraints.
Bee testicles explode after mating.
Mayflies live no more than a day.

The peacock spider's courtship dance—
—jumping, pulsating iridescent—
if too persistent, won't take no for an answer,
he's lunch.

Man is a year-round breeder, sexual appetite
exceeding one bite of an apple or need to procreate.
Female objects of his desire forced to rely on words—
consent, permission to proceed, no means no.

Poor substitutes for instincts of a female peacock spider,
venom of a dominatrix hyena or Daphne's mythic powers
of transformation—horny Apollo in pursuit—
she pleads to her father the river God,
open the earth to enclose me, change my form
which has brought me into this danger.

Life Cycle

Nothing's out of place.
The furniture hasn't moved or disappeared in the night.
The sky burdened with clouds hasn't fallen.
But the air seems thinner.
The path forward less certain,
shifted from full throttle to slow for repairs.

When I was nine,
my family moved five hundred miles south.
Alone in the back seat of our Dodge,
windows open, hot dry air and sun beating in,
I cried, leaving friends, teachers, a familiar
neighborhood park and merry-go-round,
my pet goldfish and abandoned caterpillar collection
before chrysalis and butterflies had time to emerge.

Now, decades later, I rail against loss and change, afraid
of being the last one standing in an emptying space.

Sunday Dinner

We order seasonal asparagus,
chicken in black bean sauce,
wor wonton soup, exchange
pleasantries with the waiter,
wave to a neighbor.

Small talk of weather,
granddaughter's boyfriend,
photos on the computer—
and questions:
"When were we in Prague?"

There are no helping words
after awhile,
just a swallowed tear
each time he says,
"I don't remember."

Family Gathering

They came to celebrate Papa's ninety-fourth
bearing cards, gifts and sonogram display—
"baby on the way!"
lying on its back, looking like a gummy bear,
her pinpoint legs and arms in air.

What could be better we say,
thinking back to when we were just two
who grew three,
and three married three,
who grew seven,
and together we were fifteen—
then sixteen joined,
now seventeen, an embryo in utero.

We don't have to look far for signs of age,
wrinkles, canes, aches, pains,
but you know you're old
when your first-born is Social Security eligible,
and your baby is going to be a grandmother.

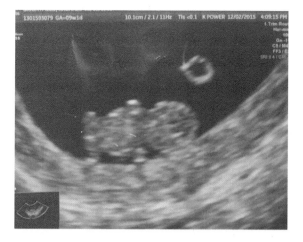

Transition

Full moon low in February's western sky—
then half, then crescent fading to white dot,
then nothing.
Out of sight, in orbit over the ridge.

Like the memorial candle there on the mantel
illuminating the room, burning for seven days,
a hundred sixty-eight hours.
Just a flicker now as I watch it go out—
leaving a tall glass cylinder empty of possibility.

My husband lived to see a thousand full moons,
ninety-five summer skies.
On clear nights we'd gaze at the galaxy,
Cygnus to Sagittarius and Scorpius,
the Big Dipper pointing toward Polaris.

I spin on my own now, from plural
to singular when "we" became "I."
No double *v* or *e* to lean on—
little things you never thought of.

Judy

My daughter has a thing for apostrophes.
She finds them in unlikely places—
gazing at my datebook, correcting misuse:
dinner with Miller's should be plural,
approving *meet me at Suzie's,* which is possessive.
I appreciate this investment in punctuation,
her talents bountiful as the dozens
of cabbage leaves she's stuffed
for tonight's family dinner.

Her daily calls, extended invitations,
leftovers supplied—watching over me
in my new role as matriarch.
I liken her to a redwood daughter,
a sentinel standing by
her mother who has fallen
for one reason or another.

Living Alone

After six decades of marriage,
friends with good intentions
suggest a pet, cat or dog for company.

I tell them I don't want to be responsible for
or worry about another living thing.
Not interested in conversing with a parrot,
watching tropical fish consume each other,
running with a mini-pig on a leash,
or changing diapers of a marmoset.

Neither does a puppy in need of rescue appeal.
As for cats, I don't fully trust them—
regression to a feral mean seems all too possible.
I'll settle for someone else's black-and-white
that strays into my garden and leaves parading
past the window, a mouse in its mouth.

I prefer passive activity—watching
a hummingbird at the feeder
warding off competitors, making rounds
to each plastic flower aperture, sucking up
liquid sweetness as she goes,

or the night herons perched in pine trees
across the creek, spreading wings to dry.
Listening to an evening chorus of Canada geese
in formation overhead, sounding like a kennel
of barking dogs, or the sudden

burst of birdsong after I scattered
and watered wildflowers and forget-me-not seeds
around my husband's newly set headstone,
marking Year One.

Elegy

Perhaps it was Mozart's Magic Flute—
Papageno's net,
the alignment of stars,
the night we met.

On the cusp of a new year,
friends gathered, played charades,
kissed at midnight and after.
The host's brother
home from medical school.

Tall, tender, trim—
quirky smile, bonny blue eyes, soft skin,
funny, and a little drunk.

Into my net there'd been
Burt who danced divinely,
George who courted with yellow roses.
Jerry who drove a convertible,
and Larry who quoted Keats and Browning—
Let me count the ways . . .

But this was different—
his touch, voice, silky earlobe.
Like Papagena, my heart sang.

From the first hello
an arrow shot straight to a vital part.
I loved him head to toe—
always in my heart, my tears, my core
and more, here or not.

Melanie Maier

"Is this when I begin to strive for perfection?"
from *Blue Angels*

Down to Earth

Shortly after takeoff
a toddler's fingers brush my arm.
A man holds her tightly.
Down below, the Rockies—
Colorado spreading, as lights
pinpoint the state that disappears.

I dwell on this: How simple
to spot endings and beginnings
at such high altitudes. Lost
so easily on the ground.

Early Morning

Granny Smith green,
the lagoon, its flat canvas
stretching just beyond our dock.
No people, just homes and hills
reflected on the water's surface.
Perfect color replicas
upside down and floating:
on one dock, two small boats
with white sails; on another,
a turquoise rubber raft neatly folded
beside red buckets waiting to be filled
and a long-necked egret stands
still as stone; looming—
browned and yellowed hills
dotted with dark green bushes
an occasional tree.
Captured too, one patch
of blue sky drifting.
A ruffling breeze
strips the canvas clean.

Birding

Desert heat rises.
A binoculared couple
sights the roadrunner,
lizard dangling from its beak.
A copper-colored hawk
puffs its feathers
and looks down at them
from the telephone pole.

They walk . . . stop . . . walk . . .
pause to rest under sycamore.
A vermillion flycatcher
flashes its brilliant chest
at his drab mate.
On the fence white-winged doves
from Mexico: they stop
in Tucson to breed.

One egg lies broken on the path.
Ants swarm the spilled yolk.

After Visiting Rumi

My bus crosses
the Anatolian plain:
scorched yellow.
Here and there
trees break monotony.
In the distance
your receding figure

walks towards mountains
shrouded in cloud.
I ache to follow.
Will these tears of mine
never stop?
My heart,
since you left,
there is nothing.

Praise

Wild parrots orange and green
shoot over red camellias

warmed by afternoon sun.
A breeze ruffles tall grass.

Spring gentles nature
softening bare branches.

Blossoms explode; sparrows trill.
Woodpeckers feed open-mouthed chicks.

In the night sky a full moon
veiled by haze.

My beloved appears
heaping praise.

Doggerel

If I were a bitch
I'd bleed for you
bite your upper lip
hold on to the softness
pull you toward me.
Growling low, I'd pant
and turn for you,
feel your breath on my neck
see how I welcome you
whimpering
as you mount
quiver
as you thrust
over & over
deeper & deeper
sperm river—
maybe a litter!

He and She

He does what former lovers
sometimes do,
follows a woman
who looks like her though
he knows it couldn't be,
propelled by a *dybbuck*
who likes to torment him…
or so he imagines.
He thinks of her,
what was and how it could be.

She wants to tell him
get lost.
Stamp his puny heart
beneath her heel
while she laughs so hard,
tears roll down her cheeks.
Talk louder, faster, longer
than she ever did before,
when he stood there staring at her
with his critical eye.

Daze

I see two roadrunners on a recent trip to Tucson. One the day we arrive, one the day we leave. To me, they're good omens.

I spend the day at UCSF waiting for Peter's ablation to be over. Our daughters and I worry. It's taking so long.

I hear a woman talking on her cell phone, *I can't deal with that right now I'm too overwhelmed.*

The robot Pug rolls by—a tall rectangular box that contains blood samples for another floor. The sign on the outside says, DO NOT BOARD ELEVATOR WITH ROBOT. Pug stops and with a woman's voice calls for the elevator. The door opens Pug rolls in. When the robot returns, I follow, it moves into an open closet and stops. Smiling, I go back to the girls.

The ablation is successful. Exhausted, heading home on the road I've driven thousands of times, I stop at a light and for a moment forget where I am.

Home, I sip tea watch the lagoon, sky, noisy blue jays pecking at our lawn and count my blessings wondering how I got so lucky.

Heart Beats

Snow looks like talc
from the air:
Chicago, buried, a frieze
in black and white—
streets, roads, freeways.

There, I begin my exorcism.
I straighten my daughter's sheets,
fold hospital corners, rearrange
knickknacks, and cook. Often,
I twist my fingers in the thickness
of her hair. Her blood spots
the white sheets. No way to stop it.

We watch videos, reminisce,
and pick names from a book.
Four hearts beat: two extant,
two in utero.
The cat, who hides, comes
and curls up next to me. Lets me
stroke the underside of her chin.

I return the way I came, flying.
Halfway home the captain asks us
to secure our seat belts
due to weather up ahead.

Eavesdroppers

Outside, crows call.
After days of gray mornings, sun.
The house—mine and the dog's—
everyone else in their rooms.
We stop at the twins' closed door
and listen to their chatter.
The dog cocks her head, wags her tail.

In a few minutes,
before their mother awakens,
I'll go in to my grandsons.
They'll pull themselves up,
hold out their arms to me.
For now, the dog and I stand
listening.

A Lecture

The marine naturalist
goes on and on.

His eyes bulge
We'll learn, he says,

and such a large head
about the brilliantly

and big feet
colored sea creatures

that live underwater.
His fingers are long, thick.

I imagine his dick, swimming
among magenta fish.

The Cape of Good Hope

I forget Rosh Hashanah
exploring South Africa.
Stranger on a cloudless day
in this part of the world
where they say

don't walk the streets after dark.
I forget the new year
in a land of screaming birds
and roaring lions.
Memory is work—

my mind wanders off
by the side of the road, where
six ostriches bathe in a pool
of brown water. Their
long feathers billow

and they turn their silly
little heads our way.
Lunch overlooks the sea.
A guitarist plays singing softly.
Famished, we eat quickly

but speak slowly this warm day.

Blue Angels

I ride the boat to Ellis Island.
I sit with hundreds in an enormous
hall on long hard benches.
Over a hundred years ago

members of my family waited here.
Uncle Sam runs the place
cleaned up for tourists: immigrant
memories—embalmed.

I hear Blue Angels, see their planes
patent-leather shiny. They fly low,
boom across the sky precision perfect
and I wonder what that takes.

A high school classmate of mine
wrecked his car speeding
on a military base. It rolled
over and over, killing his best friend.

Is this when I begin to strive
for perfection (learning some human
errors cost more than others)
sniffing it out each day?

Eight Bells

sound after the service and a four-year old whispers, *but it's not eight o'clock.* He thinks he's at a birthday party. It is, in a way, service held on what would have been the first day of the sailor's twenty-sixth year. Celebration of this life taken by the sea.

The little boy sits transfixed by the bagpiper playing before the mourners.

After the crying, the eating, the conversation, we move from San Dominican Hall outside to watch white doves. Their handler lets the boy touch a taut body, touch an outstretched wing. Twenty-six doves set free.

For Alice

Dearest girl, adieu
this dog to her grave today
in a nest of hay

        *

        *

On Jane's Napa land
Zinfandel grapes,
the family ranch,
her remaining dogs,
she tends all with care
Fire
     Fire
        Fire
she escapes   everything there
now
memory

Wildfires

Santa Rosa, Sonoma, Kenwood,
Glen Ellen, and Napa: I call
every friend I can think of.
One makes it out with her life
nothing more. Another loses
his house; others, only
mature trees, green shrubs,
bushes, flowers, gardens,
charred ruins. Thousands
dispossessed—rich, poor,
the undocumented.

A helicopter crew finds a family
who lives on a winery's grounds.
They can take out all but one.
The father makes them leave him
behind. They promise to come back
and do.
One couple, their neighborhood
engulfed in flames, clings to life
for six hours in their neighbor's pool.
Seventeen dead, fifteen-hundred structures
and thousands of acres destroyed.

The worst fires in California history.
President Trump silent.
He doesn't tweet.
He doesn't show up.

Assault

Summer 2017

You can get the blues watching our news:

Philando, Alton, Laquan—to name three
of the black men & boys
killed, senselessly, by police.

Women gang-raped, left to die in
Sudan, Afghanistan, Syria.

Death threats to Jewish community centers.
ISIS and clones—terrorist acts.

Trump's tweets spin truth to dust.

He alienates allies & wreaks havoc
with the president's job.

Charlie Rose interviews a Catholic bishop who says
the church shouldn't *numb* the poor with a promise
of heaven while it walks away with the *goods.*

My old dog walks into walls & I have
taken up talking to the dead. Grandfather Max
taught me to laugh at myself & life.

So what if he chewed open mouthed, spilled food
down his shirts & called me his *little shiksa*—

what would he think of this America?
One mind-blowing job after another,
which (by the way)

young girls give to young boys these days.

Mr. Rogers

left the neighborhood
on February 27th, 2003.
I remember how
my daughters curled into me
those afternoons
we watched him on TV.
He'd walk in the door
hang up his jacket
put on that red sweater
take off his street shoes
and pull on sneakers.
He lulled us with his starry voice
spoke soothing words
into the camera for thirty years.
He gently bolstered
the American Dream.
These days it's eroded.
These days I wish Mr. Rogers
would walk in the door again.

Angelika Quirk

"Tonight I crave the flight of ravens"
from *Angel of Repose*

Love Vignettes

I

In a city of foghorns and cobblestones
we sat in the meadow under the elm
amid yellow buttercups and clover.
He unbuttoned my blouse. I didn't mind.
Reciting Rilke: *Orpheus singt! Und alles schwieg,*
our lips moved in the belief
of clouds and abandonment.

II

My grandfather lived in a house of the dying
pinching a nurse, spilling his past
while his common-law wife of thirty years
darned socks at home
where they had raised chickens
and laughter on their balcony.

III

He kissed me behind each earlobe,
taught me rituals of happiness.
At dusk we waited for Polaris,
our voices: syncopated
melodies of the night.

IV

Tante Elsa wrote letters to Offizier Genenz
and sang songs from Schubert's *Winterreise*
before she'd disappeared, before her belongings
were mailed from a place where black smoke
rose to an impermanent sky.

V

Today I cooked his favorite meal: Rindsrouladen
and spoonfed him words of contentment,
no headlines, no rumors, no whining pain.
I stroked his forehead, surveyed his mouth,
the radiance in his eyes, and I relinquished
all fear of tomorrow's call.

Sylt

White beaches,
an island in the North Sea.
We sat naked watching
waves and sand play tag.

Sun-worshippers
when leisure
entangled hips, thighs,
and the lingering thoughts
of a place in the dunes
where we had met
in salty air breathing
seaweed, silt,
the recklessness of youth.

And you proclaimed my breast
your pillow. You whispered
promises and pronouns
of "you" and "me"
into sea shells, and I sucked in
your words with the screech of gulls.

Contours of your shoulder,
the curve of your neck,
eyes, your voice
like a song missing a note.

That night I wanted to sleep
next to you, feel your breath,
your touch, and join you
in your dream.
But the next morning:
emptiness
and idle tongues twisting.

Kleptomaniac

She stole love and pride and stuck them
like trophies on the mantel of her mind.

First was the mailman who delivered letters
on Valentine's Day. He opened his bag.
She pulled out his heart and a card with foreign stamps.

Then Pete the drummer whose red hair excited her.
She caressed the inside of his palm, snatched away
his lifeline and posted it on her timeline.

An admirer of nights and dark habits, she stole glimpses
of stars and film noirs through peek-holes in walls.

A thief of rumors and rituals, she dined on tidbits
with neighborhood spinsters and lesbian sisters
of pride parades and ransacked their yearnings
for romance and courtship.

A squatter of lofty rooms in mansions with chandeliers
and French doors, with foyers and libraries,
where in winter she moved to a suite upstairs
searching for mirrors lost in drawers somewhere.

She plagiarized Nietzsche, Goethe, and Rilke
when sending messages to God,
even though she no longer believed.

On the last page of her journal she copied
all German words that ended in "ch" like "ich"
and "mich," the hissing of her lost cat,
and pinned them to her bulletin board.

In the end she was left with gadgets and glances.
Her trophies, nesting like swallows, drilled holes
into the drywall of her brain: small openings
squinting at the hologram of her elusive mind.

To Die, to Live

Along white corridors, the smell of disinfectant, iodine,
I push his wheelchair down the ramp for the last time,
away from tubal attachments and ticking monitors,
and nurses in scrubs like floating ghosts with stethoscopes
checking his pulse, his breath, his heart. No machines,
no monitors could measure his will to die, to live.
When Father Murphy came to anoint the sick, he gave
my husband not the last rites, but the Holy Eucharist.
                              *
My father chose to live, to survive seven years in Lager 4736
somewhere in Russia. He listened to ravens pecking
on white birch: Morse code from his home in Hamburg.
And we lit candles on windowsills.
                              *
After a bout of cancer Tante Helga gave away her possessions:
her clothes to the Salvation Army, her memories to her cousin,
her songs to nobody but the wind. She refused to eat,
praying for her soul to leave the body. She believed
in the Karmic cycle, in cause and effect after the wishing bone
no longer split. At the very end she handed me her ruby ring,
red as the blood drop from her mouth when she died.
                              *
He says he wants an orange. I pick the largest from our tree,
carry it into the house like the sun after a dreary day.
He sucks on it, inhales the scent, the light:
the promise of another day, another night.

Ghosts

I want to rub their bones with valerian root,
hear the murmur of heroes and outcasts.

My mother, crazed
by the impermanence of life,
opened the gas.

My stepfather drowned
his worries in schnapps and gambled
away his license to drive. Before
the end of the war, he sank
the pistons of his ship's engine
deep into Norway's fjord,
saving his crew.

I wished I could stitch their wounded pride to their valor,
offer them songs, offer them odes.

Onkel Hans and Frau Meyer's son
killed in Stalingrad, entrenched
inside eroded graves, grappled
with the distance of home, of being reborn
if only in the minds of survivors.

One grandmother killed in Buchenwald
the other witness of Kristallnacht.
You need to grow thick skin, she'd say
and wrote in my book *Laughter is healthier
than rational thought.* When bombs blasted
she sang *In the homeland we'll meet again,*
and I thought homeland was heaven.

I must pray to them, to their haunting spirits
and in their memory plant pansies and forget-me-nots.

Broken

I wish I didn't remember that night: a full moon
                                    piercing my window, witness
                         to the birthing of my unborn dead.

Timing is everything, my grandmother used to say,   birth, death,
                                   and in-betweens linked
                   by unknowns in different time-zones, racing
                                      on a downhill slope.

There were three of them—two nameless— before Mia, my first-born.
                              One boy aborted, swaddled
                                   in blood and blame.

I no longer want to relive a past sucking   on my breast, my heart,
                                                   holding my breath,

dreaming of my mother's arm stretching   across the ocean.

But death is waiting all around us: sparrows
                         with broken necks, fallen out of nests.
I used to bury them under an ancient oak.   Or Frau Oertel's
                              rabbit raised on her balcony
                                 slaughtered at Christmas.

That's when I filled my satchel with petals and roots,   refused
                                                   to eat meat.

When Mia's hamsters died, first one, then another,   she stuck
                              crosses on their graves.
                           The next day she asked:
                              Will you die? Will I die?

I didn't believe in heaven, or eternity.   My parents
                        used to quote Nietzsche, or was it Marx?
Religion das Opium des Volkes.   Yet at their funeral
                        Pastor Hansen read their eulogy.

But I admit, I needed a crutch,   so when Mia asked again and again:
Is it true that I will die? Is it true?   I told her
                        of a place in the clouds.

We collected leaves and wrote notes   addressing God. At night
                        we set them ablaze

sending smoke signals skyward.   I held her hand, and we watched
                        amber sparks like stars ascend.

Prague

2018

That day we lost our way in the alleys of the Jewish Quarter
trudging from one synagogue to another where names
of Holocaust victims scrawled on walls stuck to my soul,
blemishes of my forefathers there to stay.
Voices from loudspeakers: hissing rollcalls
of the dead, all marked absent.

A drawing by ten-year-old Hana Ziegrova of a princess
stabbed by a dragon. Sobs and moans drifted
from the Moldau, from the arches, the plazas, the towers
where chimes clocked in this hour.

We needed angels! We needed redemption!
And on the Charles Bridge where thirty saints stood watch,
we rubbed their silver armor for good luck while beggars
from Bulgaria crouched, their heads touching the ground.

The next day we climbed up the old castle steps in search
of Kafka. There, perched against the ancient wall:
his tiny studio at Golden Lane No. 22. He wrote
"Metamorphosis" there in the quietude of night,
slithering downriver way after twelve escaping
the characters of his own creation.

Between the Church of the Holy Spirit and Spanish Synagogue
he now sits in his black suit and bowler on the shoulders
of a headless man, his gaze fixed, pointing a finger straight at us.

That night I dreamed of a giant cockroach crawling into my bed,
and when I screamed, Kafka whispered in my ear:
Murder me! Murder me!

Cruising the Danube

We sit mid-ship sipping red wine and laughter,
pleasure-seekers, geezers, gawkers, hipsters, imposters,
on a boat, on a trip floating, cruising downriver.

A gypsy flirts with my lover from Melk to Vienna,
past monasteries where monks had dug tunnels to nunneries.

Let's leave behind the mist of centuries. Let's roam
the hills of the Viennese Woods where Beethoven lost
his hearing but found Elise, where winds rustle
with ancient gossip from canopies to sky to castle.

River of blue waves, she flows, she heaves, she sighs,
she waltzes by. I yearn for Linzer Torte in coffee houses,
for Viennese balls and try to grasp the essence of loss.

Our next stop Budapest: eight hundred Jews shot to death,
their empty shoes left ashore, their bones sinking,
their blood running backwards.

River of sobs, she moans of wars, of loss, and currents
dividing lands lap the shores in foreign words.

Merrymakers, sun-worshippers, widows, spinsters with tickets
to the end of the trip, to the mouth of the river.
Lounging on deck they listen to their own chatter
inhaling bloody Marys, rumors, and the rush of water.

After he left me for the redhead, the one with the voice
of a canary, I decided to get off before sorrow
could swallow me and pull me under,
before shipwrecked, before the end of the journey,
the Black Sea.

Mein Vater

I hardly knew him. He was Karl Palm, father of Parker, Ingrid, Gunnar, and me. This is his story:

He left the house before I could remember. Holding me, holding on to the times of belonging, after Hitler's shrill rambles, after roofs collapsed hitting his very essence. A pacifist, he refused to join the NAZI party, refused to display swastika flags.

In the first year of war he was drafted. He put on his uniform, his boots. Ingrid saw him off: how he joined his battalion, how he raised his right arm, then goose-stepping in unison with the others, he marched away down Borsteler Chaussee. She wiped her tears and waved. He never turned his head.

He was a medic, followed the wounded to the Russian Front, amputated arms, legs, feet, and his memory of fear. During the Russian winter frostbite nipped his lips, his words. He was captured in a field hospital. First, the sound of machine guns, then the groans of a few survivors—nothing else.

After seven years in a prison camp in a small town in the Ukraine, he returned. I remember sitting on his lap, on his bloated belly smelling his uneasy breath, the silence in his voice. He bought me a porcelain doll that could open and close eyes, took me to a play. But I avoided calling him Papa.

Before the war he was a modern dancer with Lola Rogge. In a medieval procession of *Totentanz* (Dance of Death), he roamed through the aisles of Lübeck's cathedral in death-defying circles. A Wandervogel, a sun-worshipper, he hiked barefooted in the heath, the naked beach of the island of Norderney, playing his harmonica. He rode his bike through the streets of Hamburg, through the windswept passages of his life, never back pedaling, always in forward gear.

After his return he pretended to be strong, yet his eyes
said differently. They toiled with the questions of Heimat,
Familie, a roof over his head since my mother now lived
with another man in the house they once shared. In the
middle of the night he would scream, then wake up in
terror from dreams of the wounded and dying.

He came to my school during third grade. I hid under my desk.
Thought he would kidnap me as my mother had said.

His pockets stuffed with postcards written to his mother,
unread, returned with her belongings from Buchenwald
after she was killed. He stooped under the weight, but always
tried to pick up his pace, stubborn, determined.

At his funeral, still wandering in search of a permanent place
among overcrowded tombstones, he was moved from one
grave to another. Finally laid to rest, not next to his cousin
Helmut, but stacked on top of a stranger. Last time I visited
his grave I heard a rustle in the leaves. Was it his restless spirit?

He visited me twice in California. Yet even then I hardly knew him.
But on the Day of the Dead I take his harmonica from my shelf,
the one he gave me, and play *Die Vöglein im Walde*,
his favorite song.

Fourteen Steps Down

to the basement, brick walls oozing
dampness where earwigs hid in crevices
among potatoes dug up in the fields,
in the heath, hoarded by my brother
and sister in the summer after the war.
No longer children playing in the streets,
they learned the trade of thievery
during the time of starving bellies.

They carried them to the wagon,
in heavy burlap sacks and backpacks,
stow-a-ways on a train to Niedernstegen
to the cellar once a bomb shelter
where we used to hide,

fourteen steps down.

My mother peeled and grated
the raw potatoes to prepare the batter.
Then take it over to our neighbor,
to Frau Hoppe's electric stove.
The gas in our unit was turned off
every other day.

Just thinking of these potato pancakes,
topped with applesauce with fruit
from our Schrebergarten,
even now makes my mouth water.

But I still remember my childhood nightmare
of men with potato heads,
eyes popping out and stalks clawing
claustrophobic ceilings, sending
white tendrils after me through the dim light,

from fourteen steps under.

Magrittomania

Inspired by Yuri Possokov's ballet

I dreamed I met him in Paris
in the Jardin Tuilleries
in his black overcoat, his top-hat
silhouetted against the green.

What was hidden under his bowler?
A dove, a peasant dance?
The French revolution?

As he tips the brim does it lift
to a Mad hatter's convention?
To his lover's shrouded head
sashed with grief?
To his mother floating downriver?

Or is he tipping the brim of his mind
to a girl in red, flaunting a green apple,
keeper of seed and birth?

A giant apple, an orb rising
with Magritte's thoughts: the absurd,
the concrete, the personal:
Everything we see hides another,
and the room is listening.

But when the giant apple rises,
then suddenly pops midair,
we are at a loss. A cheap coup de grace?
A blow to our hatless minds?

They Are Dancing

They are dancing the tango, the samba, the hula, the mambo,
thrusting legs, slicing air with arms, with tambourines, red scarves,
and fiery eyes. Rocking, bopping their heads, stomping their feet.
Swaying, swooning, lost in the beat.

Dancing in the middle of the world stage filled with confetti
and grief, dancing in carnival parades with red ribbons, batons,
balloons. And on their mother's grave next to a gate to enter, to exit.

Tap-dancing on wooden planks, dancing in halls, in barns
in straight lines to a fiddle slightly out of tune. Breakdancing
on sidewalks, in plazas, in alleys in Harlem. Dancing among derelicts
in a park, as bullets ricochet near a bar, as couples dance
at the inaugural ball. Shadow-dancing with the sun, winds blow,
leaves cling to twigs like fugitives waiting for the right breeze.

Some women dance when soldiers return: mothers, lovers, wives.
Others dance on poles in clubs collecting dollar bills in bras,
limbs undulating like snakes, curling up, and hissing.

Maypole dances, weaving strings, celebrating spring.
The Dance of Death in Grace Cathedral along aisles,
below arches, near the baptismal font, near the cross.

They are skipping along sidewalks to follow the piper's call,
his flute, his charm, and in the end they fall, singing, holding hands.

They were dancing when Beethoven sang *Ode to Joy,* when Hitler
wrote *Mein Kampf,* and the Manhattan Project was done.
They are still dancing when bombs blast, faces stained with blood,
when shots hit the innocent child. And when they are born:
first cries, then kicking legs.

They touch the sun, then dance on ashes, practicing the graceful
ways of angels. They dance on shards of a broken world. They dance.

Chasm

I have been where the wisteria climbs
the latticed fence and on the beach
tossing brittle shards into the forgiving sea.

I have been in my studio:
self-portraits staring, amber paint
dripping down blank walls.

And I have been in my bedroom,
his warm breath enticing
our thighs to interlock.

But when I entered last night's dream
holding the stallion's black mane,
riding toward the edge
where tectonic plates clash
from east to west,
from laughter to sorrow,
from order to chaos,
I stalled

and at this great divide
I saw a grid of lines, my town,
with trenches and fences
where my roots had outgrown their soil.
I wanted to wake up
and not be thrown
into the chasm below.

Monologue with My Self

I
When I awake in the morning,
my thoughts drift
like shadow dancers of the night before,
once hiding in crevices and corners,
now showing off with boisterous voices
on the blank walls of my room.

I need coffee and the scent of rosemary
to face today's affairs,
and yesterday's prognoses.

I don't want spirits of the deceased
grinning through the open shutters
mocking me and dawn unwilling
to give up its mist.

II
Yet I need a fix: cracks in my ceiling,
smudges on my windows.
I wrote a letter of complaint
to an invisible god about children dying,
about my psyche running amok,
about my inner eye, my ego, my id
slipping away last night.
Should I check on them
in the nearest psych ward?
The nearest morgue?

III
At this early hour there is nothing left:
no patience, no bargains. Only a broom
to sweep ashes and dust under a rug.

This and That

Not every Sunday asks for sermons,
for bells ringing, among a multitude of voices,
riding the slippery road to salvation.

                    *

Let's pray for the next generation and be thankful:
we have each other, the hand of a handyman,
a house retrofitted for disaster, the fortune teller's
prediction for a long life, the testimonial of a midwife
who heard our first cries, survivors of famine and war,
war crimes repudiated, guilty conscience cleansed,
stained clothes sent to the cleaners,
a living will, a will to live.

                    *

Today I compiled a list for my heirs:
a list of praise, a list of this and that.

                    *

And I yearn for the innocence of laughter
and tears. I want to hear the gibberish of toddlers,
feel the origin of joy. So I watch my two-year-old
granddaughter at play, giggling
when her dog licks her face.

Phases

Der Mond

He-moon rises above the horizon.
I spy on him through my double-glass
window over suburban Hamburg,
a sickle about to slice the sky in two.

Fifteen nights later he grows
full and plump flooding the sky.
Floating over Paris,
nouvelles attitudes,
his name now

La Lune

She-moon brags, she swells,
courting clouds to wear their gowns,
mimicking lovers on the Seine
that bathe in her reflection.

Der Mond – La Lune

peddler of dark dualities,
lusting mysteries,
on a quest, lost
in a war of personas.

Tonight in the desert of my mind
I will hear again Coyote's howl
at the orange light.

He-moon, new moon, she-moon, full moon
staring back—silent.

Angel of Repose

Between remnants
of Sunday sermons
and my conscience,
your voice is audible
like the creak
of a door that moves
when the wind blows.

Brushstrokes of mauve
watch from my ceiling
when on Mondays I share my bed
with a man. He puts roses
on my pillow I feel his breath
on my face,
yet your whispers
from behind pillars distract.

I live in a world of skittish winds
and shifting hands
a world of wildfires and neon lights,
and my cat has fleas. In the dark
your halo shines:
a crescent moon lopsided.

Today my phone rings,
my faucet drips and drips,
but then during the night
when the Ghost Ship burned
to the ground, when 36 charred bodies
were carried out.
there was your deadly silence.

As a child I used to lie on the ground
brushing wings onto the melting snow.
Tonight I crave the flight
of ravens.

he was outside

outside the brick wall   outside the door   the warmth
of room   of floor   where the cold nipped his lips
and puffs of air rose with each sigh   outside
with shuffling steps   losing his footprints in the mud
after the war   after he had taken off his boots   his badge
then walked into the river   then changed his mind
he was an outsider   a clock-stopper   rattler of gates
and laws   outside of his mind   of gestures of kindness
and lucky strikes   a recluse of words and songs   he was
outside   crouching in doorways   freezing   dreaming
of a thousand beginnings

he was from the wrong side of the river   the dumpster
where he disposed of his rags   his rage   his shoes
his memory   even his shadow   tired   hungry   he was ready
to walk the alleys   the tunnels   the hills   dreaming of a street
with open doors   to find an entrance   maybe to a church
a school   or a waiting room   at a bus stop   to take off
from there   to somewhere   maybe to the girl   who still wore
the ring he had given her   before the war   before she shared
her bed with another   before she changed the lock
or to the dealer of dope   to whom he had offered his soul
now he wanted it back   in exchange for a token   his bronze
star   his pistol   or his kidney   or maybe he could return to his
childhood home   his neighborhood   where his mother
would stand   in the threshold   with open arms   but he no longer
remembered   his own address

Gabrielle Rilleau

"*Agree with me now, it's time to let go*"
from *Gathering*

Dance

Dance man dance
Move it out of safety
Into chance
Touch it with romance

Roll it into neutral
Slip it into first
There you go
Feel the flow
Dance man dance

Now you slide it
Out of first
Ease it into second
Cross the crowded floor

Take her by the arm
Twist her under yours
There you go
Where who knows
Dance man dance

Past those men
In business suits
Ladies with their high-heeled hoots
Hold her 'round her waist

Out the door
Down the street
Never know
Who you'll meet

Do not fear
The music stopping
Let the band play on
Dance man dance

Don't just sit in repetition
Of wash the dishes
Clean the kitchen
Pass the mashed potatoes

Dance man dance

Enter Death

My Mother's Passing

We kept watch as Death made entrance
upon her body
I slept the nights on her old
sleeping bag spread
upon the floor beside her bed

The youngest daughter slept upstairs
The other children, close family
came for final visits

Talk was minimal

Death slowly stepped between us
then took the upper hand

In those thirty days
and nights
all those long hours
as the moon shone through her window
with its radiance and solitude
reflected on the bay
we only spoke of life

First Jobs

When I find myself
in Walgreen's, CVS, or Longs,
the smell of stale popcorn and cheap cosmetics
instantly throws me back half a century
to age twenty, Boston, Boyston Street, to J. J. Newberry's
serving vanilla cokes
and to St. Johnsbury, VT, to Ames Discount Department Store
ringing up $3.00 ladies' shoes and men's $4.57 pants.

In those days I walked a tightrope in fear
of being pulled down a road
where polyester slacks and plastic flowers were my destiny,
a road my parents had done their best to steer us from,
The New Yorker and *Harper's Bazaar* always about,
my father, a tailor's son, pointing out the importance
of the French seam on a well-stitched shirt.

Somehow I escaped.

But those earlier years—one tentative step at a time,
balancing that taut line along aisles
of Whitman's Chocolates, bundles of packaged socks,
cans of off-brand peanuts, and bottles of blue perfume—
left their mark.

Knowing

It is good to know something well
To know it very well
In a way you can count on

Like the moon
What the phases are
Which side fills up first
And where it will be in the sky

Or the tide
To follow its course
To know how it will rush in around the flats
And when it will be high

And it is good to know you
Your routine
The way you walk in the door
Bend down to pet the dog
And call out my name

It is good to know these things well
To be able to count on them
The one
Then the other

Gathering

Remember our starting
way upstream
with few belongings
and a dream?

Before the house
before the truck
you simply had a TV, a car and a dog

I had a place back east
a TV, a car and a kid
neither of us
was looking for anything more

I had thoughts
of moving back east
but your eyes were so blue
I never looked away

You became the best of fathers
to that thirteen-year-old boy
I did pretty well
for that dog of yours

At some point we started collecting
things we didn't need
along this river
It's getting to be quite a heavy load

My forearms are cramped
from the years of our gathering
Agree with me now
it's time to let go

It is time for our shedding
so we can hold something new
something lighter
Let's find out together what it is

Gabrielle Rilleau • 93

Getting Close

I know there is an opening
I've felt it in rare moments
but it closes so quickly
and when it happens
I am always on the outside

This morning you come with candles
to light the way
I follow
brushing cobwebs from the passage
mindful that some easy breeze
could extinguish the flame
as has happened
time and time again

High Five

Some days
When life seems overwhelming
I take my days in fives

I make five phone calls
Put five articles of clothing away
Pay five bills
Throw away five things in the refrigerator
Pull five weeds
Plant five plants
Give my husband five kisses
And go to bed by five p.m.

Loving You

When it comes to the words which say
exactly what I feel in loving you
to find the words I trust your ears
would hear or eyes would read
precisely as I mean
with not a single word left out
and not an extra word thrown in
to gaudy up the easiness
of all I feel for you

When it comes to finding these words
it is a search
I expect to continue
my life's remaining days
always seeking the perfect way
to say everything I mean

When it comes to loving you

Now

We both lean forward
in our walk of late
        a reaching
        a bending down

I put a quarter
into the tiny porcelain dish
high on the shelf
        my wager for a future

The phone rings
It goes unanswered
I want no intrusion
on ocean's whisper in my ears
        an incessant call since childhood

There is so much more than this
it tells me
And there is nothing else

Between the rains
I am called to turn the soil
That moist down-to-my-depths smell
of all that has gone before us
all that has leaned forward
        and finally folded into the earth.

On the Honeymoon

I meant to say
before we shoved off
that this boat
has a few holes
It leaks here and there
And I meant to tell you
there is a storm due
sometime soon
And oh yes
I meant to say
I do not know
how to sail
But I can swim
I meant to ask
Can you swim too?

R.E.M.

You found your way
into my sleep once more
As always
saying so little
Everything
by innuendo

Silence
I suppose to be taken
as some token
of understanding

No naming of names
Both paralyzed
by the unspoken
Such cowards are we
to meet
only in each other's dreams

Saturday Afternoon

If I take in the details
with every step
in this last little jaunt from the mound
of strawberries needing fresh additions
past the bearded iris
on the downside of their season
through the arched jasmine-covered gate

giving it the extra tug to hear
the click of its slightly rusted latch
taking in the barren garden beds
waiting for planting
where oregano is staking claim ·
by the old iron bedrail on hold for some proper use
as it leans against the aging fence

take in the smell
from the bucket full of freshly picked lemons
to be sent to my sister's Greek neighbor
who longs for the days of her own lemon tree
back home and to Ruth who makes
special preserves and curds
in her tiny kitchen while she longs
for her little dog Pierce
who began biting her
in final stage of aging

If with every step
I observe and serve—
quiet myself down
and do the tasks at hand—
I believe I will get through
any burden that felt too much
at the day's beginning

The Art of Deception

I took the poet at his word
Or perhaps I mistook
the poet for his words
spoken in eloquent mystery
lulling me into
a magician's illusion

Fatal mistake

All I saw was what I wanted to see
All I heard was what I wanted to be

Fool am I
for I certainly know
just as the emperor has no clothes
so the poet shuffles his words.

Too Early the Morning

The day has come too early
I return to sleep
where thoughts
are shuffled into submission
under direction of a wild magician
fanning double-sided yesterdays
fashioned with illusion
throttled with time
the twine that binds it all

Third Grade

I tell my mother I do not remember third grade.
Most other years I remember,
but my memory of Mrs. Nickerson
and third grade is very sparse.

I say *it was a disheveled time in our lives.*
We were a disheveled family my mother responds.

Mrs. Nickerson *was kind of awful* she says.
And asks if she was the teacher that sat on top of our desks.
No I tell her. That was Miss Welch.

Mrs. Nickerson was the one with a hunch back
and was quite gentle.
Her husband was a photographer
for *The Cape Cod Standard Times.*

The thing I do remember from third grade
is the Dick and Jane reader.
Then the memory stirs of my mother, after school
sitting at one of the small desks
in the back of the room
Mrs. Nickerson in the one next to her.
They are talking about me.

Later that day my mother tells me
Mrs. Nickerson had complained I was incorrigible
for taking my Dick and Jane workbook home
to work at on my own.

My mother scoffs at the accusation
of any third grader being incorrigible,
shakes her head and with a smile
says, *In the future, just leave Dick and Jane at school.*

What the Child Holds

He is sitting at the kitchen table
We are the only ones in the house
I see him take a swig from his half-pint

You know, he says slowly
head on a slight tilt, looking straight at me
The reason I drink . . .
And there was a pause
       I think the reason is finally coming
       so then we can fix it
The reason I drink is . . .
and he slowly took a deep breath
I cannot stand
to be with myself

We look at each other
There are no further words
I am a child
Knowing this reason
does not ease . . .
It does not ease at all
my helplessness
my grief

Your Shoes

I look at your shoes today
long and narrow
hold one in my hands
smell the sweet mixture
of light sweat and fine leather

My fingers move slowly
across the soft worn surface
you've so carefully rubbed
with brown Kiwi over the years

I've heard your firm footsteps
quickly up and down our stairs
along concrete sidewalks
briskly down the street
watched your long stride
across our wooden floors

By the swirls
on the ball of the sole
I see most of your turns have been to the right

You've walked life at an angle
against the wind
I love you
my left-handed man

Sock Rags

After years of wear
a pair
of his black socks
has holes in the heels

Over time
he wisely purchased only
socks of the same brand and color
so when one goes
the other still has a useful future

Today I decided that two socks must go

The first I cut quickly across the middle
just above the ankle
which gives me two decent wipe rags
for small jobs

At the second sock I pause
give more thought to the years
this cloth has covered my husband's foot—
feet to be precise
as certainly he has worn it on each foot
over the years

A quick cut across the middle seems so mundane
so up I go to the cuff
come the long way down the back
to the heel
where it begins to thin
at the offending hole
shearing through the sole of the sock
and ending at the toe

As I unfold it each time I dust
I have a beautiful bat-like rag
to fill me with contented thoughts
of this man I love

Where I Want to Be

I ask myself
what I contributed
to this day

I hugged warmly
with joy
and no intention
two women I hardly knew
because I loved their faces
painted with hard work
and simplicity

It would have been
a greater contribution I believe
to have hugged
two people whose faces
repelled me

This tells me
I have a long way to go
before I get
to where I want to be

About the Authors

Ella Eytan began to keep a notebook of poems at the University of Chicago while she was earning her BA. She had even written a few poems in high school, but became serious about her writing around 1980. She served as co-chair and newsletter editor to the Marin Poetry Center during the organization's formative stage, and started their anthology which continues to this day. She organized and led, in addition, a number of poetry retreats to Asilomar for the Center.

Ella has two books of poetry—*Haying the Far Fields: Poems on a Minnesota Childhood* and *After a Certain Age*. She finds writing poetry a way to un-layer complexity to arrive at underlying truths. It is, in fact, a spiritual practice and a practice in excellence for her. Also, there is the sheer joy of the process and the exhilaration when she produces a good poem. She has been published in a number of journals such as *Seattle Review, California Quarterly, Barnabe Mountain Review,* and *Poet Lore.*

Laurel Feigenbaum was born and raised in San Francisco and then Beverly Hills. She holds a BA in English Literature from UC Berkeley and an MA in Educational Research and Psychology from San Francisco State University. After family and careers in education and business, she gathered what she refers to as "late life courage," and began writing. She credits Wordsworth and her father as sources of her interest in poetry. Her father loved word play and often quoted lines he admired or found useful. Her book shelf is now home to his *Synonym Finder, Complete Rhyming Dictionary,* and Roget's *Thesaurus.*

For Laurel, writing is a way of coping with the often absurd world in which we live, and with the inevitable changes that occur in living a long life. Her work has appeared in *Nimrod, Highland Park Poetry Challenge, Les Femmes Folles Anthology of Women Poets, December, The Marin Poetry Center Anthology,* and *Voices Israel.* She has served on the board of the Marin Poetry Center, and published a first book, *The Daily Absurd.*

Melanie Maier was born and raised in San Francisco. She earned a BS from UC Berkeley and a JD from UC Hastings. She practiced law in San Francisco and in Marin County before retiring to write poetry.

Melanie's poetry has been published in reviews such as *The Fourth River, phoebe, Southern California Review,* and *The South Carolina Review,* as well as in *Gazeta Wyborcza,* in Warsaw, Poland. Her first chapbook, *The Land of Us,* was published by Pudding House Press. She is the author of two other chapbooks, *Scattering Wind* and *Night Boats,* and two full-length books of poems, *sticking to earth* and *Invention of the Moon,* all from Conflux Press; and a co-editor and contributor to the anthology *Chapter & Verse: Poems of Jewish Identity,* also from Conflux Press.

Nothing gives Melanie more satisfaction than the time she takes writing poetry. She considers it her spiritual practice.

Angelika Quirk was born and raised in Hamburg, Germany. At 18 she immigrated to the United States. A dancer, a teacher, an artist, a lover of music, a collector of words in German and in English, she has written poems about people and experiences going back to her German roots. Her Leitmotif is to instill true emotions and passions from the surreal to the sublime, from chaos to rhythm and rhyme. Two of her books, *After Sirens* and *Of Ruins and Rumors,* are on display at the library of the German American Heritage Museum in Washington, DC.

She writes about herself:

If a person's life could be compared to a tapestry interwoven and embellished by different experiences, my design would stand out for its vivid colors, and for the intricacy of patterns juxtaposed from early childhood on, when I grew to adulthood in war-torn Germany moving between two cultures, dancing in Totentanz *and* Ode to Joy, *raising three children, and coming to terms with "the German Question," looking into the mirror, searching.*

Gabrielle Rilleau has lived in Marin County for over fifty years. She joined the Marin Poetry Center in 1996 which she credits with awakening the sleeping poet within her.

Gaby was raised on the tip of Cape Cod, where she returns twice annually for a nourishment that is fodder for many of her poems. In her home there she has hosted small, week-long retreats for women writers in the spring and fall for seventeen years.

In addition to the poems in this anthology, Gaby's collection of Provincetown poems is close to "being born," though she says it may be a cesarean. For decades, Gaby has studied under the masterful tutelage of Tom Centolella and David St. John as well as having benefited from the wealth of fine poets in the San Francisco Bay Area.

Acknowledgments

Some poems were first published, sometimes in a slightly different version, by these presses and journals:

Conflux Press, *Invention of the Moon*: "Praise," 2015
Cyclamens and Swords online: "Weekends, Sea Ranch," 2013
December: "Transition," 2018
FicusFig Tree Press, *The Daily Absurd*: "Donatello's *David*," "*Double Delight*," "Life Cycle," "Sociology," "Sunday Dinner," 2014
Ina Coolbrith Circle: "Matrimony," honorable mention, 2015
Marin Poetry CenterAnthology: "Broken," 2018; "Living Alone," 2018; "Weather Report," 2016; "Message," 2012
Nimrod, Lasting Matters Anthology: "Gertrude, The Stein Collection," 2013
Plainsongs: "To Die, to Live," an award poem, 2018
Poetry Sunday Women for Change online: "Words and Music . . . ," 2016
Talking River: "The Memory of All That . . . ," 2013
TRANS-LIT2: "Kleptomaniac," translated into German and published in bilingual fashion, 2015

blurb